creARTivity

create.art.activity

GOLD & SILVER
SNOWFLAKES & STARS

Illustrated by **Cindy Wilde, Eyizera Phoenix, Hannah Carby & Melissa Castrillon**
Written by **Elizabeth Golding**

RP | KIDS
PHILADELPHIA · LONDON

Make amazing art with gold and silver gel pens

This book is jam-packed full of fabulous things to draw with silver and gold gel pens. There are extra goodies in the pack attached to the book, such as paper stencils. You can use any gel pen, as well as those that came with this book. Let's get started!

There are so many ways to use gel pens! Try out these ideas.

Draw big spots.

Make zigzag scribbles.

Draw criss-cross shapes.

Draw horizontal wobbly lines.

Make short vertical marks.

Draw spiral shapes that touch.

Draw lots of tiny dots.

Draw loose circular scribbles.

Draw overlapping diagonal lines.

Make vertical lines.

Draw diagonal lines.

Draw wide zigzags.

Draw wave shapes.

Draw little squares.

Draw overlapping lines in gold and silver.

Make marks in gold and silver.

Make a 3-D picture frame

There are two 3-D picture frames to make. One has a printed gold frame and the other is blank for you to color as you like. The frame has two parts: a back and a front. Gently press out the pieces and glue your favorite piece of art to the back. Hang up your picture with sticky putty.

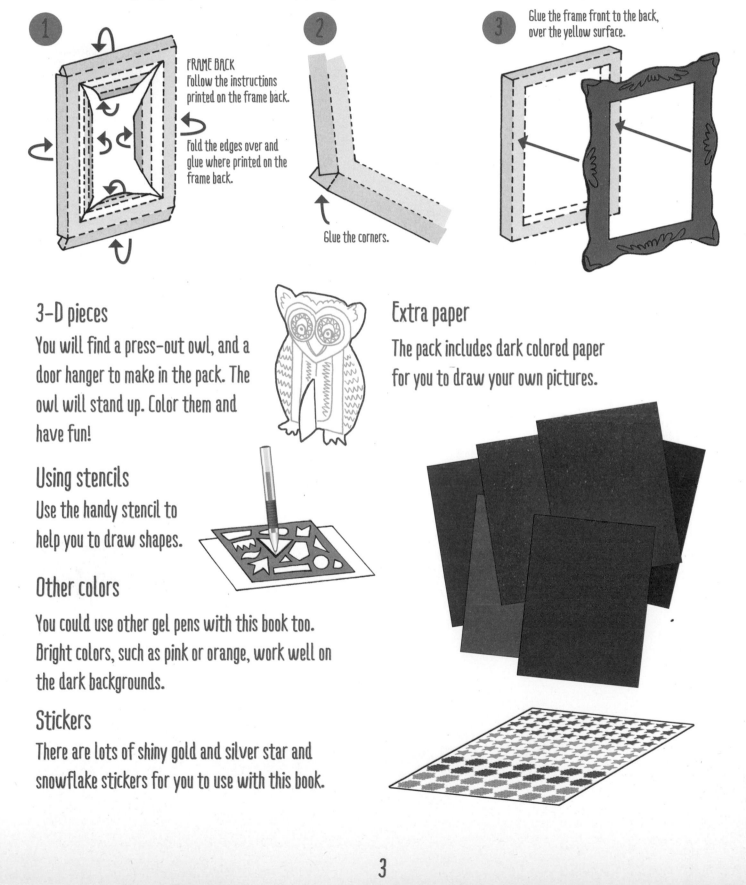

1

FRAME BACK
Follow the instructions printed on the frame back.

Fold the edges over and glue where printed on the frame back.

2

Glue the corners.

3 Glue the frame front to the back, over the yellow surface.

3-D pieces

You will find a press-out owl, and a door hanger to make in the pack. The owl will stand up. Color them and have fun!

Using stencils

Use the handy stencil to help you to draw shapes.

Other colors

You could use other gel pens with this book too. Bright colors, such as pink or orange, work well on the dark backgrounds.

Stickers

There are lots of shiny gold and silver star and snowflake stickers for you to use with this book.

Extra paper

The pack includes dark colored paper for you to draw your own pictures.

What might be in this snow globe? It's up to you!

Complete the other **half** of each unfinished **snowflake**.

Use the **stencil** to add more **snowflakes.**

Sprinkle the **buildings** and **sky** with **snowflakes.**

Who turned out the lights? Decorate every house and finish the windows.

Light up the night sky
with silver and gold.

Scatter **the sky** with beautiful *silver* and **gold** snowflakes.

Remember, every snowflake is different!

Draw the rest of this palace in *silver* and fill in with *gold*.

Fill the star tree forest with silver birds, flowers, and stars.

Finish drawing the silver fox.

The silver fox needs some friends. Draw another fox and some cubs.

Draw lots of leaves in different shapes and fill each of them with a swirly, icy pattern. How many can you draw on this page?

Fill the rest of this *page* with gold stars of every kind!

Connect these **spinning** Catherine wheels with **gold** and **silver dashes**. Add flying **sparks** too!

These little **robins** are caught in a **snowstorm!**

Draw the **swirling** snow!

Draw the rest of this silver lovebird.

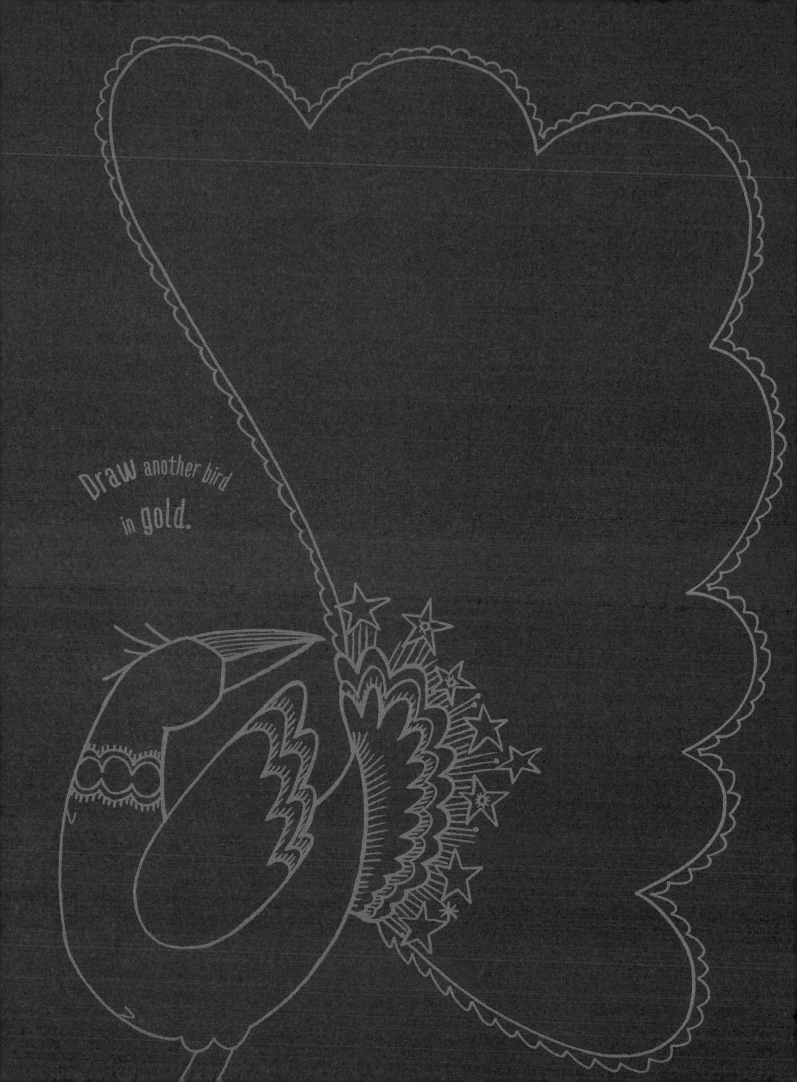

Draw another bird in gold.

Continue the rest of this scene with penguins, snowflakes, and fish.

Sweet dreams! Imagine the rest of this dream catcher!

Penguins and polar bears never meet!

One lives in the Arctic and the other in the Antarctic. Find out which is which at the bottom.

Penguins live in the Antarctic, in the Southern Hemisphere. Polar bears live in the Arctic, in the Northern Hemisphere.

Draw snowflakes, penguins, and footprints in the snow. Use a black pen for the penguins' backs.

*

Draw a silvery moonlight masterpiece! Imagine waves on a wild night. Draw the sea, a boat, and lots of stars. There are stickers too!

Draw stars and snowflakes around this winter tree.

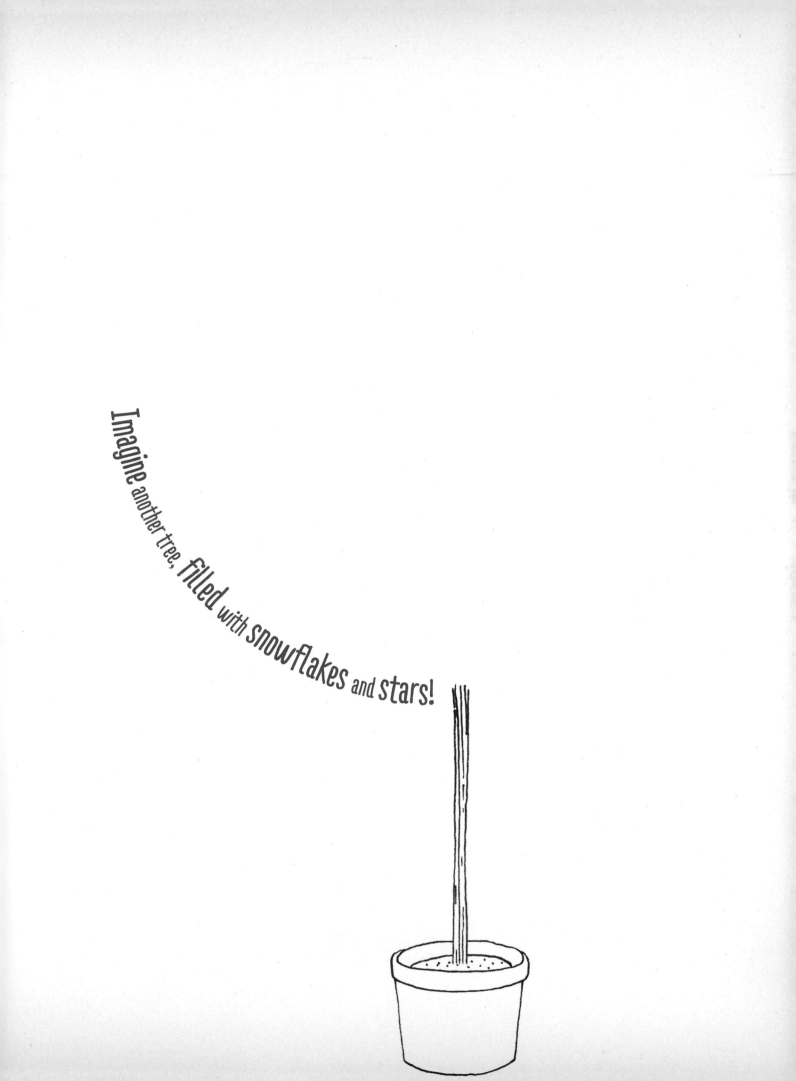

Imagine another tree, filled with snowflakes and stars!

Draw **lots** of silver starfish in the submarine **light**.

Add **gold** creatures too!

Use **gold** and *silver* to make **patterns** on the **ornaments.**
Add some extra **ornaments** too!

We are the **moonlight** animals!
Fill the **scene** with silvery **stars** and **patterns**.
Finish the animals too.

Connect the different groups of dots to see the creatures of the night sky

Imagine and draw a lovely pattern to fill the small space

The Northern Lights have lit up the sky!
Make a silvery pattern with snowflakes, stars, and squiggly lines!

Finish drawing **golden houses** too!

Draw a **magical forest** filled with **stars** and **snowflakes!**

How many ways can you draw a star?
Draw a different silvery star in each blank space.

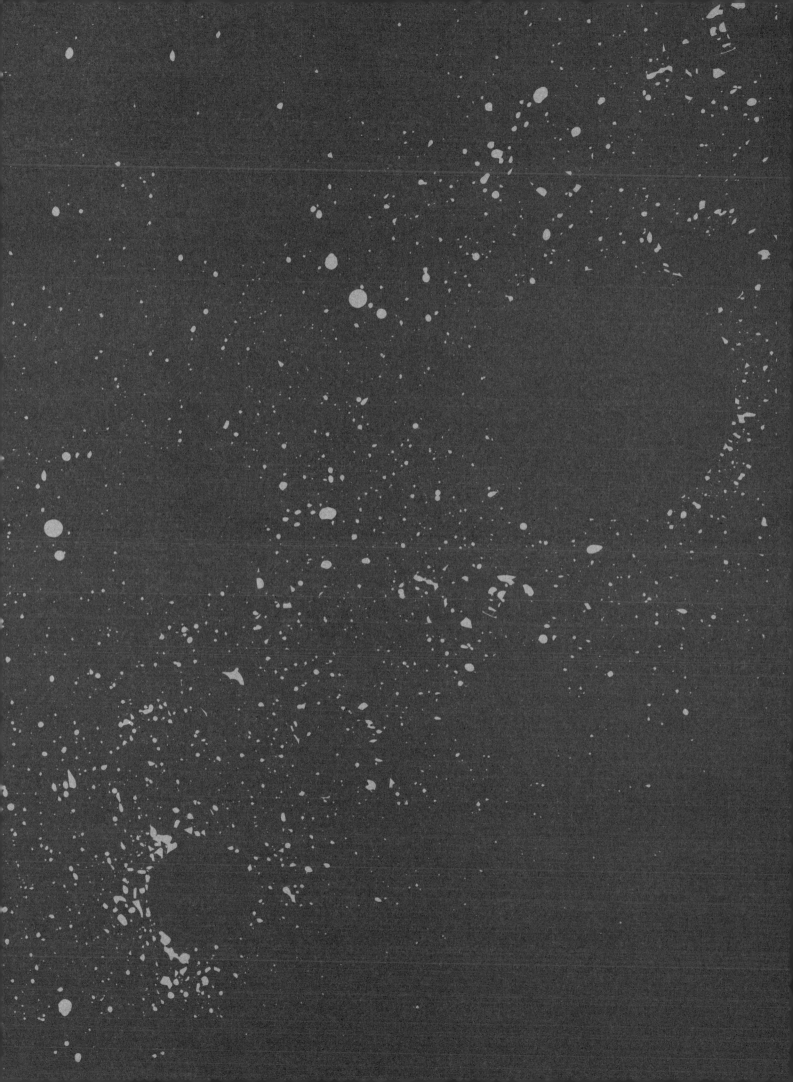

Grow fantastic flowers and plants, using stickers, stencils, silver, and gold!

This family of snowy owls has starry eyes.

Finish all the owls with **silvery** stars and lines.

Knit this sweater like crazy with stars, squiggles, and snowflakes!

Imagine the **winter palace** in a **snowstorm** and fill the sky with *silver* snow!

Make a **golden plume** with lots of **little stars** for this **phoenix**.

The Ice Queen is coming through a snowstorm, wearing a silvery crown.

Draw a beautiful crown with sensational stars!

The snowstorm is swirling! Add lots of snowflakes, large and small!

Draw double silver stars for the owl to catch in the sky!

Draw the wolf and the rock.

Fill the sky with silver stars.

Just have fun! Fill this page with **gold stars** and **snowflakes**.
Add some *silver* **snowflakes** too!

Created and produced by **iSeek Ltd**
Illustrated by **Cindy Wilde, Eyizera Phoenix,
Hannah Carby & Melissa Castrillon**
Illustration elements by **Shutterstock.com** : SkillUp, hfng & Mejnak
Written by **Elizabeth Golding**
Designed by **Anton Poitier**

© 2014 by iSeek Ltd

Books published by Running Press are available at special
discounts for bulk purchases in the United States by
corporations, institutions, and other organizations. For
more information, please contact the Special Markets
Department at the Perseus Books Group, 2300 Chestnut
Street, Suite 200, Philadelphia, PA 19103, or call (800)
810-4145, ext. 5000, or e-mail
special.markets@perseusbooks.com.

ISBN 978-0-7624-5623-9

9 8 7 6 5 4 3 2 1

Digit on the right indicates the number of this printing

Published by Running Press Kids
An Imprint of Running Press Book Publishers
A Member of the Perseus Books Group
2300 Chestnut Street
Philadelphia, PA 19103-4371

Visit us on the web!
www.runningpress.com/kids